## INTRODUCTION

### You bought a bass...so now what?

Congratulations! You look great holding that new bass, but won't your friends and family be even more impressed if you can actually play the darn thing? In just a couple of weeks, we'll have you playing some cool riffs, as well as jamming on some full songs. By the end of this book, it's on to the hits—the Beatles, Clapton, Hendrix, and more.—in the *FastTrack* songbooks.

All we ask is that you observe the three Ps: **patience**, **practice** and **pace yourself**.

Don't try to bite off more than you can chew, and DON'T skip ahead. If your fingers hurt, take the day off. If you get frustrated, put it down and come back later. If you forget something, go back and learn it again. If you're having a great time, keep on playing. Most importantly, have fun.

## ABOUT THE AUDIO

*G*lad you noticed the bonus material—audio tracks! Each music example has been recorded so you can hear how it sounds and play along when you're ready. The examples are preceded by a one-measure count-off to indicate tempo and meter. Hal Leonard's *PLAYBACK+* allows you to emphasize the guitar part by panning right, or the accompaniment by panning left. This symbol will indicate an audio track is available for the example:

Speed • Pitch • Balance • Loop

To access audio visit:
**www.halloonard.oom/mylibrary**

Enter Code
**2512-0696-4578-9219**

ISBN 978-0-7935-7408-7

Visit Hal Leonard Online at
**www.halleonard.com**

Contact Us:
**Hal Leonard**
7777 West Bluemound Road
Milwaukee, WI 53213
Email: info@halleonard.com

In Europe contact:
**Hal Leonard Europe Limited**
42 Wigmore Street
Marylebone, London, W1U 2RN
Email: info@halleonardeurope.com

In Australia contact:
**Hal Leonard Australia Pty. Ltd.**
4 Lentara Court
Cheltenham, Victoria, 3192 Australia
Email: info@halleonard.com.au

# PARTS OF THE BASS
## *What a beauty!*

Below is a standard electric bass. Get acquainted with the parts of your bass, and, heck, give it a name if you want. You'll be spending a lot of time together.

head

tuning keys

nut

neck

frets

fingerboard

position markers

body

pickups

tone/volume controls

output jack

bridge

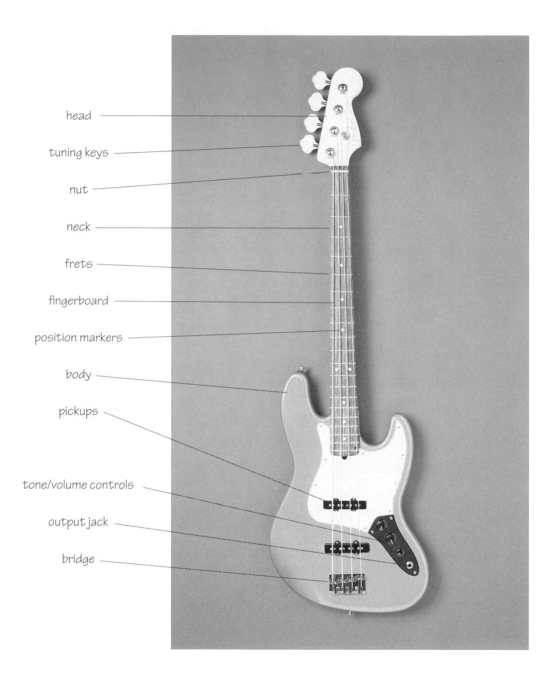

# TUNING

When you tune, you correct the pitch of each string. **Pitch** means how high or low a musical tone is. This is adjusted by tightening (or loosening) the string, using the tuning keys on the head of the bass. The tighter the string, the higher the pitch.

Your four strings should be tuned to these pitches (low to high): **E-A-D-G**.

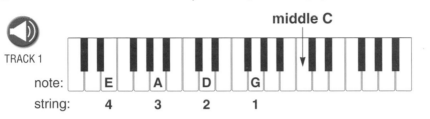

TRACK 1

CAUTION: Tighten slowly and not too much, or you'll be heading back to the store to buy new strings!

## Piano tuning

No, you aren't about to tune an entire piano! If you have a piano or electric keyboard nearby, play the above notes one at a time and tune the corresponding string until its pitch matches that of the piano.

## Electronic tuner

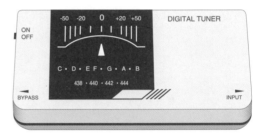

If you don't have the luxury of a piano or keyboard, you may want to purchase an electronic tuner.

A tuner will "listen" to each string as you play it and indicate whether the pitch is too high or too low.

Don't give up hope—If you don't have a piano and you can't buy a tuner, there's yet another solution…

## Relative tuning

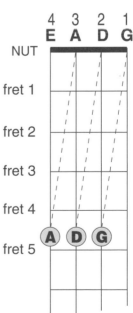

To tune your bass by ear, you must tune the strings to each other. This is done in the following manner:

**1** Assuming string 4 is already E, press string 4 behind fret 5, play the depressed string 4 and open string 3 together. Adjust the pitch of string 3. When the two sounds match, you're in tune.

**2** Press string 3 behind fret 5 and tune open string 2 to it.

**3** Press string 2 behind fret 5 and tune open string 1 to it.

# A FEW MORE THINGS
## (...before we jam!)

## Playing Positions

**P**erhaps the most comfortable and least tiring way to learn bass is to sit while playing.

Once you learn a few tunes, feel free to stand up. But for now let's put that extra effort to better use—playing.

sitting

standing

Hold the neck of the bass with your **left hand**, with your thumb resting comfortably behind the neck.

Hold the neck slightly upwards—not downwards (at least not until you're on stage in front of thousands of fans).

left hand position (fingers)

left hand position (thumb)

There's nothing stressful here, so don't grip the neck too hard (you might strangle it!).

# Strings & Frets

**Fingerboard diagrams** (or "grids") picture a portion of the fretboard and show you where to play the notes. Circles with note names are drawn onto the diagram to indicate the notes played.

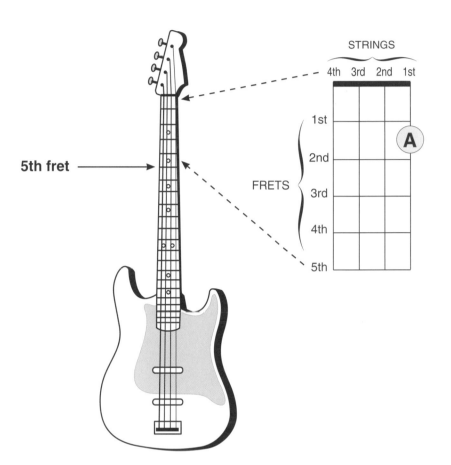

**5th fret**

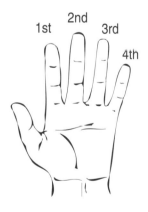

Think of your fingers as being numbered 1 through 4.

# DOG-EAR THESE TWO PAGES

*(...you'll need to review them later)*

fold ↖

Music is a language with its own symbols, structure, and rules (and exceptions to those rules). To read, write, and play music requires knowing all the symbols and rules. But let's take it one step at a time (a few now, a few later)...

## Notes

Music is written with symbols called **notes.** Notes come in all shapes and sizes. A note has two essential characteristics: its **pitch** (indicated by its position on the staff) and its **rhythmic value** (indicated by the following symbols):

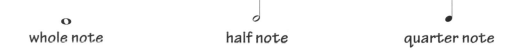

whole note                half note                quarter note

The rhythmic value lets you know how many beats the note lasts. Most commonly, a quarter note equals one beat. After that it's just like fractions:

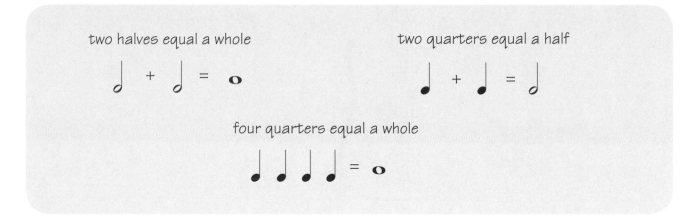

two halves equal a whole                two quarters equal a half

four quarters equal a whole

## Staff and Clef

All the notes are written on (or nearby) a **staff,** which consists of five parallel lines and four spaces. Each line and space represents a different pitch. A symbol called a **clef** indicates which pitches are represented. A **bass clef** staff makes the lines and spaces have the following pitches:

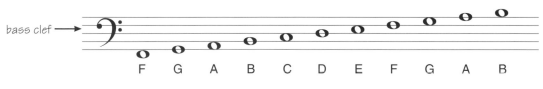

bass clef →

F   G   A   B   C   D   E   F   G   A   B

## Leger Lines

Since not all notes will fit on just five lines and four spaces, **leger lines** are used to extend the staff:

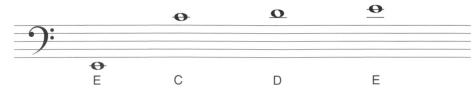

E       C       D       E

## Measures (or Bars)

Notes on a staff are divided into **measures** (or "bars") to help you keep track of where you are in the song.

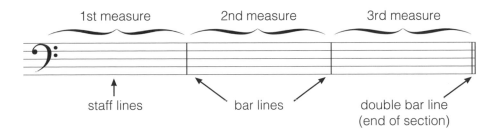

## Time Signatures (or Meters)

A **time signature** (or "meter") indicates how many beats will appear in each measure. It contains two numbers: the top number tells you how many beats will be in each measure; the bottom number says what type of note will equal one beat.

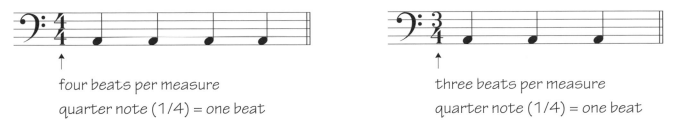

four beats per measure
quarter note (1/4) = one beat

three beats per measure
quarter note (1/4) = one beat

## Tablature

**Tablature** (or "TAB") is a specially designed staff for bassists. The four lines on a tablature staff represent the four strings on your bass. A number is placed on a line to indicate which fret to press.

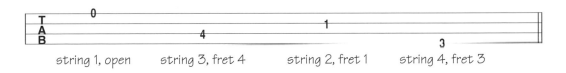

string 1, open        string 3, fret 4        string 2, fret 1        string 4, fret 3

IMPORTANT: Tablature should be used simply as a guide. You should still observe the notes, time signatures, and rhythmic values written on the music staff.

By the way, all of the music examples in this book use both a staff and tablature to make playing easier.

☞        **R**elax for a while, read through it again later, and then move on.
(Trust us—as we go through the book, you'll start to understand it.)

# LESSON 1

## *It's time to play something!*

If the left hand "selects" a note by depressing a string at a fret, what does the **right hand** do? The right hand actually plays the strings, but you have three choices of how to play with the right hand:

### 1. With a pick…

Because of its more accented sound, this is a preferred method of playing by many rock bass players. Hold the pick in your right hand, as shown, and attack each string:

Pick with **downstrokes** (attack in a downward motion) or **upstrokes** (attack in an upward motion).

Using all downstrokes with your pick, play four beats on each open string (meaning don't press any frets):

## Open Strings

TRACK 2

### Picking and Grinning

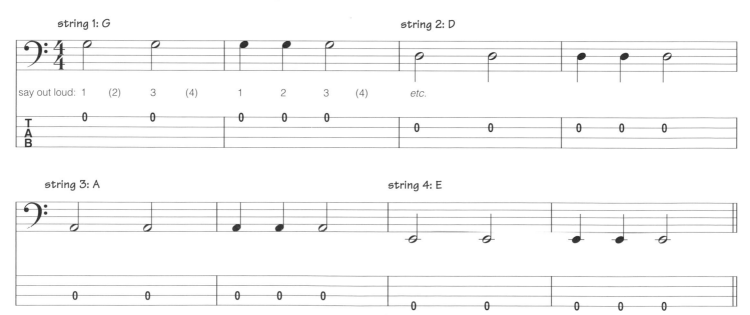

Try the same example again but use upstrokes.

## 2. Fingerstyle playing...

This is the traditional way of playing and allows you more control (since your fingers can feel where to go). Rest your thumb on the **pickup** and play the strings with finger 1 (your index finger).

After you play a string, let finger 1 rest on the next string up. For example, play string 3 and rest finger 1 against string 4.

**IMPORTANT:** Don't let your right-hand fingers "curl up." Notice the relaxed position in the photo above.

### Fingerstyle Practice
TRACK 3

NOTE: After playing string 4, you can rest finger 1 against the body of the bass.

## 3. Alternate fingers...

A third (and faster) way to play is to alternate between fingers 1 and 2. Keep your hand in fingerstyle position (thumb resting on the pickup) and play string 3 once with finger 1, then once with finger 2:

### Two-Finger Jam
TRACK 4

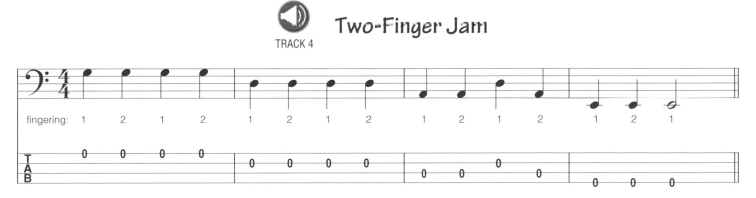

YOUR CHOICE: Choose the right-hand playing style that's the most comfortable and best-sounding to you.

# LESSON 2
*Start at the top...*

## Notes on the G String

You've chosen a playing style. You know all the open strings. And you're eager to play. Let's get down to business...

**String 1: G**

Forget strings 2-4; let's concentrate on string 1 for now. Use the photos and fingerboard diagrams below to play your new note A.

You just learned it, but it's worth repeating. Here's the open string G:

Play string 1 while pressing fret 2 with finger 2 and you hear A, which lies just above G on the staff:

Practice your new notes. (If you need a quick review of rhythmic values or time signatures, flip back to pages 6 and 7.)

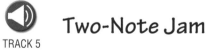

**Two-Note Jam**

TRACK 5

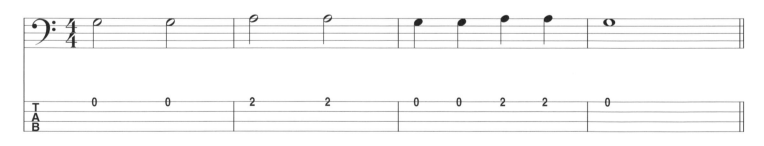

☞  "What happened to fret 1?" That note is A-flat. We'll explain **flats** later.

NOTE: We realize that you already learned another A (open string 3 on page 8). But since the musical alphabet consists of only the letters A through G, this type of repetition will eventually occur with all notes.

Play string 3 open, followed by your new A:

## Same Name, Different Note
TRACK 6

Sound similar? The new A sounds one **octave** higher than open string 3. An octave means eight notes apart. Bass players play lots of octaves, so get used to this new concept.

## Put it to good use...

Just like reading a book, you should be going to the next line in the song as soon as you reach the end of each staff. However, when you see this symbol (  ), you are at the end of that song.

## My Sharocka!
TRACK 7

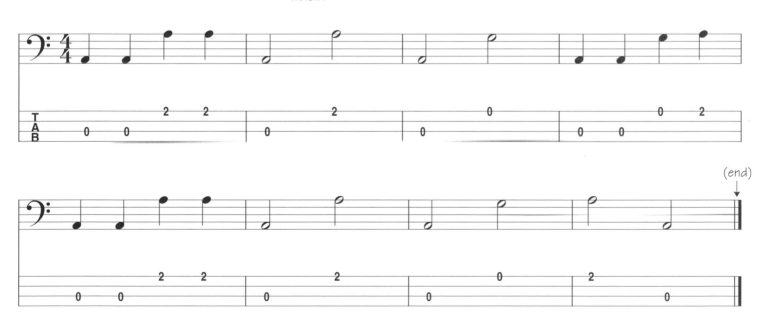

(end)

# SOME MORE NOTES ON MUSIC
## (...pardon the pun!)

*B*efore going to Lesson 3, we want to tell you some more about the hieroglyphics of music.

## Rests

A musical **rest** is a pause. Rests are like notes in that they have their own rhythmic values, instructing the musician how long (or how many beats) to pause:

| whole rest | half rest | quarter rest |
|:---:|:---:|:---:|
| (four beats) | (two beats) | (one beat) |

IMPORTANT: A rest does not mean rest your fingers or put your bass down! During a rest you should get your fingers into position for the next set of notes.

## 🔊 Take a Load Off

TRACK 8

say out loud: 1    2    (3)    4    (1  2  3  4)    1    2    (3  4)    1    (2    3)    4

PLAYING TIP: During a rest, practice **muting** the strings with your left hand (so there is no sound).

## 🔊 Rock, Roll, and Rest

TRACK 9

12

# LESSON 3
*Moving on...*

## Notes on the D String

Take a few seconds, flip back to page 3 and make sure your bass is still in tune.

**String 2: D**

 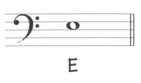

A quick reminder of open string D:

D

Now play string 2 while pressing fret 2 with finger 2 and you get E:

E

Press fret 3 with finger 3 and hear F:

F

Time for another workout. (Practice slowly and count out loud!)

**TRACK 10**    **D-E-F**

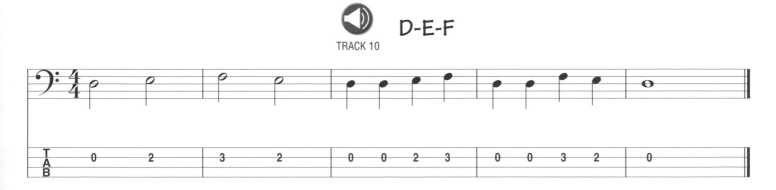

When you feel comfortable with D-E-F, try them in combination with your other two notes...

**CHANGING STRINGS**: When changing fingers from string 1 to string 2, try to let your eyes move ahead in the music, and your finger move to the correct string before the next note occurs.

TRACK 11

## DEF Jam

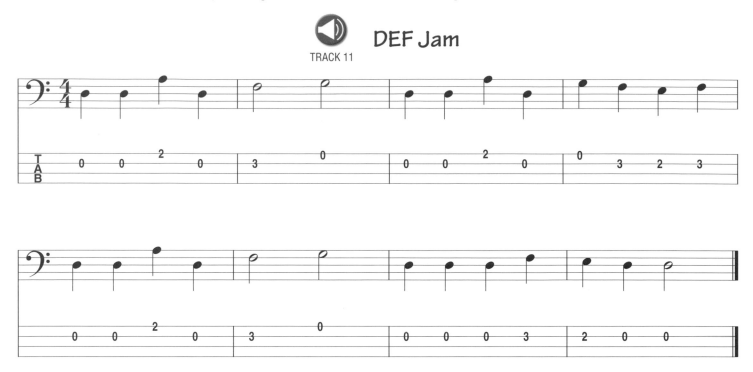

HELPFUL HINT: When playing a higher note, leave the lower note depressed. For example, leave finger 2 on E while pressing finger 3 on F. When you go back to E, simply lift finger 3.

TRACK 12

## Bass Boogie

*Repeat these examples at least twice more, playing a bit faster each time.*
*When you're ready, we'll move on to Lesson 4.*

# LESSON 4
*A little lower now…*

## Notes on the A String

Unbelievable—five notes already. You're a fast learner! How 'bout another string? (Make sure you're still in tune, if not—page 3.)

(Make sure you're still in tune, if not—page 3.)

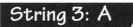

### String 3: A

String 3 is exactly like string 2 (except it's thicker):

Don't forget the open string is A:

A

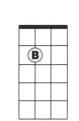

Press fret 2 with finger 2 and you get B. (Keep those fingers arched!):

B

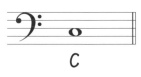

Press fret 3 with finger 3. That's C:

C

Here is a practice tune.

TRACK 13

## A-B-C Rock

15

Now play all the notes you've learned...

TRACK 14

A to A

Do you realize what you just played? That was your first musical **scale**—A minor!

## What's a musical scale?

Scales are arrangements of notes in specific patterns of **half steps** (one fret apart) and **whole steps** (two frets apart). Most scales have eight notes with the top and bottom notes being an octave apart. The one you just played started on A and used a **minor pattern**, thus it was the A minor scale.

Try this bass line that's built on the A minor scale...

TRACK 15

Rockin' Riff

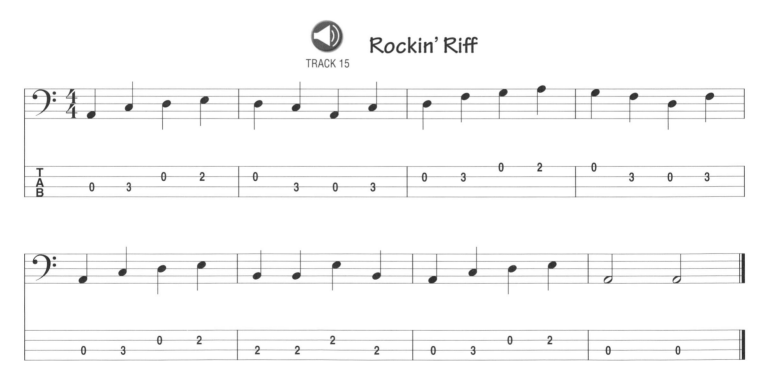

Scales are essential to bass players! They're the basis for all your riffs and licks. We'll learn many more scales throughout this book, but for now...

# YOU GOT RHYTHM

## Ties & Dots

### Ties

A **tie** connects two notes and tells you to hold the first note through to the end of the tied note:

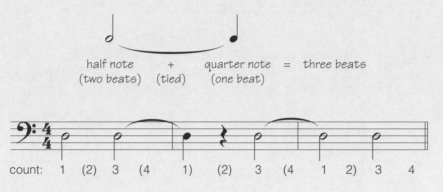

### Dots

Another way to extend the value of a note is to use a **dot**. A dot extends the note by one-half of its value. Most common is the **dotted half** note:

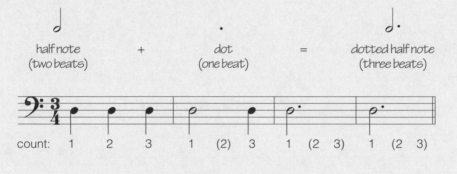

Try some bass lines with ties and dots...

TRACK 16    **Extend This!**

Remember to count out loud until you begin to think and feel the beat.

# 3/4 Time

CAREFUL! The next one is in 3/4 meter. That is, there are three beats per measure. (For a quick review, flip back to page 7.)

## Rockin' in Three

TRACK 17

Back to 4/4 meter (or four beats per measure)...

## Fit to Be Tied

TRACK 18

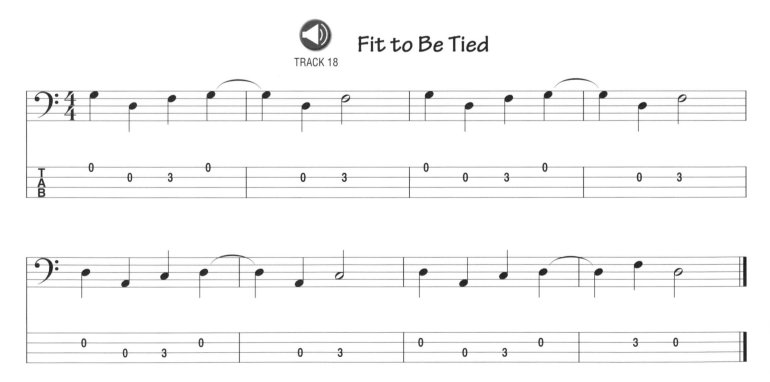

Excellent! But can you do it faster? Are you playing along with the audio?

TRACK 19

## Crosswalk Blues

# Repeats

**Repeat signs** have two dots before or after a double bar line ( ║⁝    ⁝║ ). They simply tell you to repeat everything in between. If only one sign appears ( ⁝║ ), repeat from the beginning of the piece.

TRACK 20

## Good Team Spirit

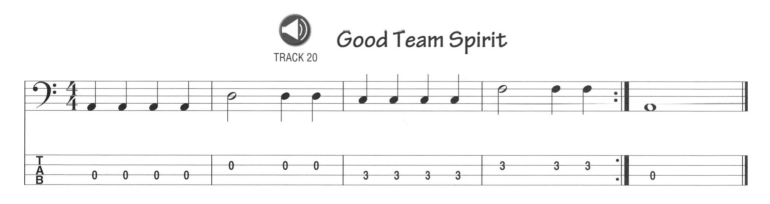

☞ This is a good time to take a break. Then come back, review Lessons 1-4 again and continue with Lesson 5.

# LESSON 5
## *Down to the bottom...*

## Notes on the E String

Let's check your progress: three strings and eight notes. Now we'll tackle another string...

### String 4: E

This time you get to play fret 1 and skip fret 2 (we'll explain why in the next lesson)...

 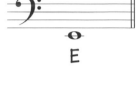 Of course, open string 4 is E:

 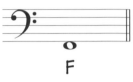 Wake up finger 1, press fret 1, and you get low F (your second F, so far):

 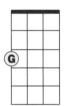 Skip fret 2 and press fret 3 with finger 3 (careful, it's a stretch!). That's low G:

Turn it up and let's rock with these new low notes...

 E-F-G

TRACK 21

Remember the A–A octave? Now you know four octave pairs.

**Octaves Apart**

TRACK 22

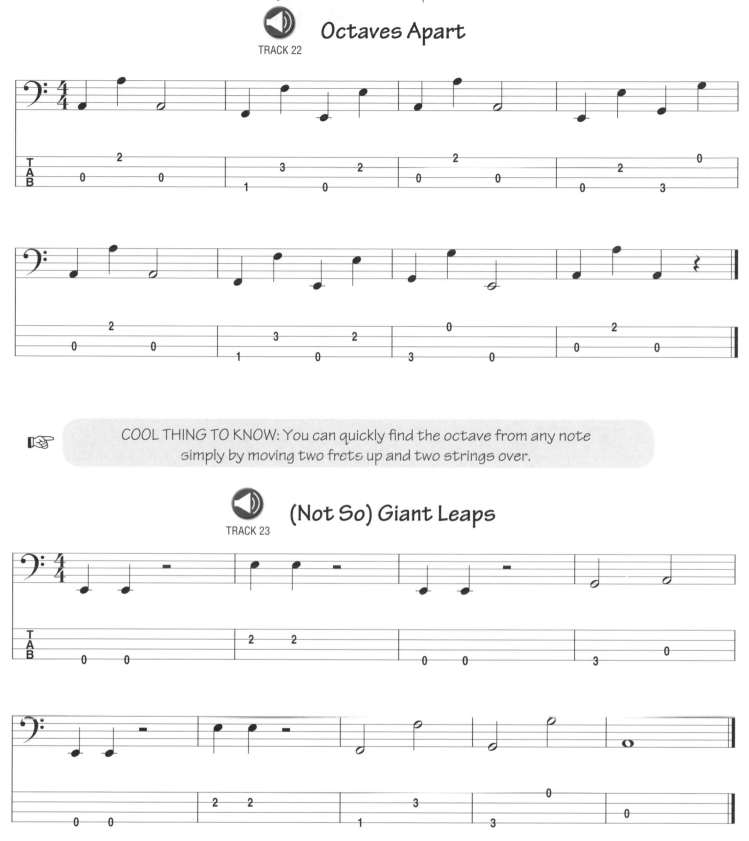

COOL THING TO KNOW: You can quickly find the octave from any note simply by moving two frets up and two strings over.

**(Not So) Giant Leaps**

TRACK 23

If your fingertips hurt, take a break. But never fear—the more you practice, the faster they will toughen up.

# YOU STILL GOT RHYTHM

## Eighth Notes

*Can you spare a quarter? How 'bout an eighth?*

An **eighth note** has a flag on it: ♪

Two eighth notes equal one quarter note (or one beat in 4/4 and 3/4). To make it easier on the eyes, eighth notes are connected with a **beam**:

To count eighth notes, divide the beat into two and use "and" between the beats:

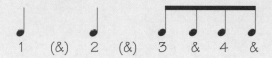

Practice this by first counting out loud while tapping your foot on the beat, then play the notes while counting and tapping:

## Eighth Rests

*What about the rest?* ♩

**Eighth rests** are the same, but you...pause. Count, tap, play, and pause with the following:

Now try a bass line with eighth notes. (Keep that foot going!)

### Eighth Note Rockin'

TRACK 24

Excellent. But don't stop there…

# Pickups

Instead of starting a song with rests, a **pickup measure** may be used. A pickup measure simply deletes the rests. So, if a pickup has only one beat, you count "1, 2, 3" and start playing on beat 4:

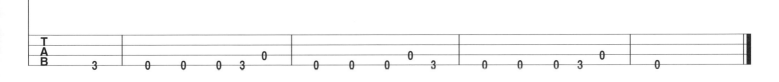

Try these riffs with pickup measures:

## Pickup and Jam

TRACK 25

Watch out for the eighth-note pickup in the next song, and remember to mute the strings during the rests...

## Sneakin' Around

TRACK 26

☞ *Remember to practice slowly! Speed up the tempo only as you become more familiar with the notes.*

# LESSON 6
## *The notes between...*

## Sharps & Flats

### Why we skipped those frets...

As we learned on page 16, music is made up of **half steps** and **whole steps**. When a song requires a note to be only a half step higher or lower, a symbol is placed by that note.

One half step higher is called a **sharp** and looks like a tic-tac-toe board: ♯

One half-step lower is called a **flat** and looks like a lower case "b": ♭

EXCEPTION TO THE RULE: From E to F is only a half step; from B to C is only a half step. (Look at the white keys on the piano diagram on page 3.)

We'll learn two notes we skipped earlier—a sharp and a flat:

  On string 4, press fret 2 with finger 2 and play F-sharp:

 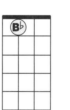 On string 3, press fret 1 with finger 1 and play B-flat:

### Groovin'
TRACK 27

24

## Sharpening Groove

TRACK 28

As promised, here's another "sharp-looking" scale:

## E Minor Scale

TRACK 29

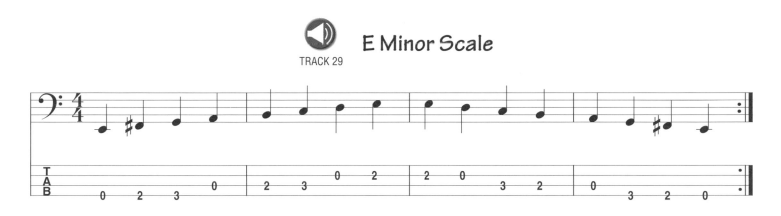

Repeat the scale again and then try a riff based on it (careful, the riff is in 3/4 and has all eighth notes):

## E Minor Riff

TRACK 30

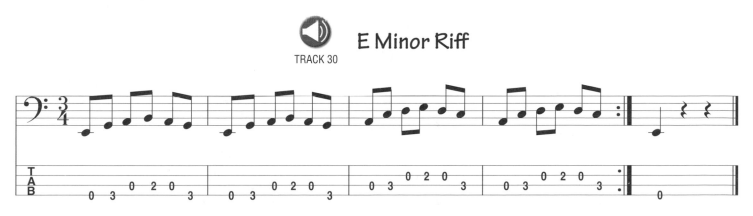

Wow, those fingers can really move! Practice and practice some more.

Now for another scale—one that uses the flat you learned:

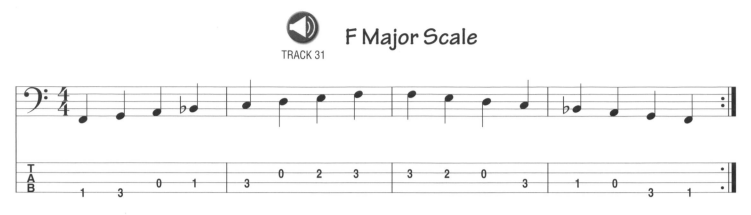

Congratulations! That was your first **major** scale (we'll explain later). Try a groove and a song based on the F major scale:

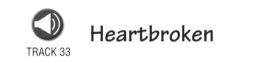

NEW RULE: A **natural sign** (♮) cancels a sharp or flat on a note, returning it to its natural pitch (but only within that measure).

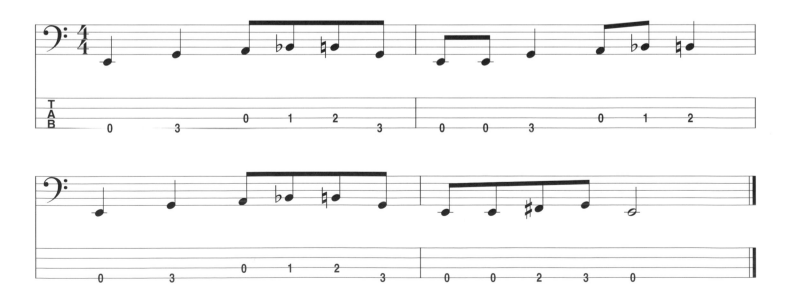

# What's in a Name?

Two things give a scale its name: the scale's lowest note (called the **root** note) and the pattern of whole steps and half steps used. (For a review of steps, flip back to page 16.)

## Major vs. minor...

As you can see (and hear), a major scale is no bigger (or any more important) than a minor one, it's just a name. The real difference between the two is the specific pattern of half steps and whole steps used to create the scale. These patterns can be used to build scales on any note.

Here's are illustrations of the major and minor scale patterns:

TRACK 34

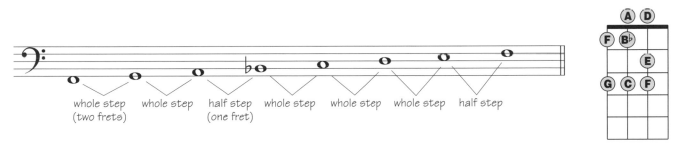

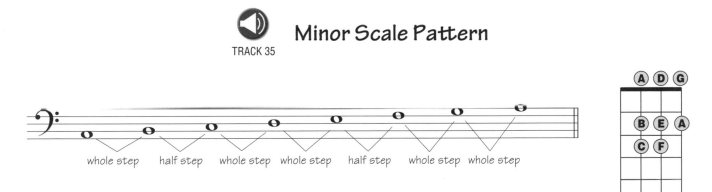

LEARN IT BY EAR: Without checking the pattern,
you can hear the difference between a major and minor scale.
Put simply, a major scale sounds "happy;" a minor scale sounds "sad."

# LESSON 7
## *Almost forgot...*

You want more notes? Here are two more notes we skipped on fret 1 earlier...

**Notes: E-flat and A-flat**

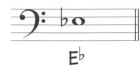

On string 2, press fret 1 with finger 1 and play E-flat:

E♭

On string 1, press fret 1 with finger 1 and play A-flat:

A♭

TRACK 36    More Rock 'n' Roll

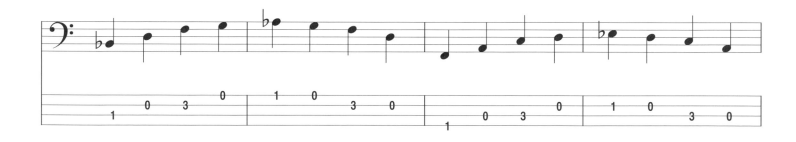

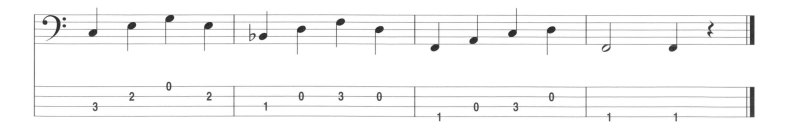

28

# Dotted Quarters

Remember the dotted half note (three beats)? A **dotted quarter** note gets one and a half beats:

| quarter note | + | dot | = | dotted quarter note |
|:---:|:---:|:---:|:---:|:---:|
| (1 beat) | | (1/2 beat) | | (1 1/2 beats) |

Think of it as being like a quarter note tied to an eighth note.

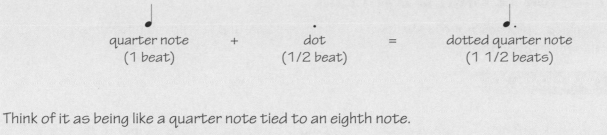

count: 1 (&) 2 (&) 3 (& 4) &    1 (&) 2 (&) 3 (& 4) &

Listen to the next two examples while you clap the beat. Once you can feel the rhythm of the dotted quarter, try playing it.

### Ballad Style

TRACK 37

### Dusty Road

TRACK 38

This was a short lesson, but DON'T RUSH! Take your time and review it again.

# LESSON 8
*Know your roots...*

## Root Notes & Chord Symbols

As you learned, the **root note** is the lowest note of a scale, and the note that names the scale. Roots also name **chords**...

**What's a chord?**

Chords consist of three or more notes played simultaneously. **Chord symbols** (like the ones below) are written above the staff, indicating which chords are being played in each measure.

Listen to some examples of chords:

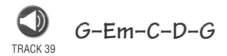

TRACK 39    G–Em–C–D–G

## Accompanying chords...

Although bass players don't normally play chords, it's essential to know about them, since your bass lines will use the notes of the chord being played.

Play track 39 again. For the next song, you'll play the root note of each chord symbol...

### Rootin' Around

TRACK 40

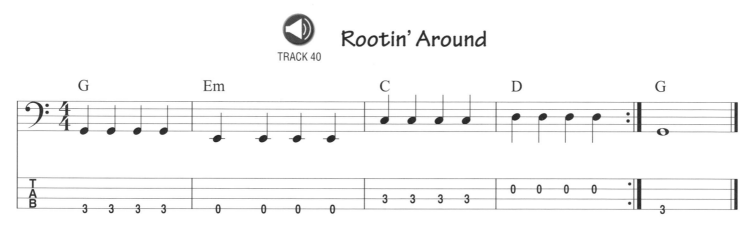

Try varying the accompaniment rhythm on the same type of song.

### Rhythmically Rootin' Around

TRACK 41

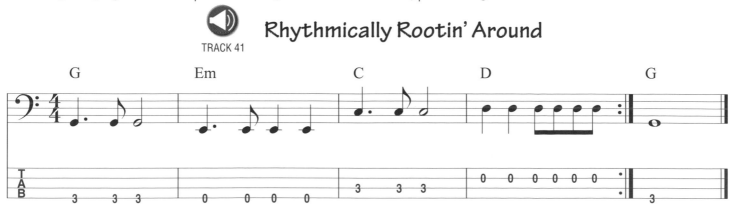

*A bit faster now…*

## Some Fast Rootin'

TRACK 42

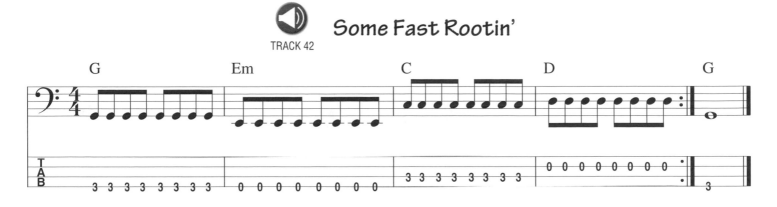

Here are several more examples of root note accompaniment. Just follow the chord symbols…

## Punk Groove

TRACK 43

## Heavy Rock Groove #1

TRACK 44

## Heavy Rock Groove #2

TRACK 45

In addition to the root note, you can use other notes of the scale to create your bass lines…

## Octave…

Interchange the root note with an octave higher or lower…

TRACK 46

## Jumpin' Bass

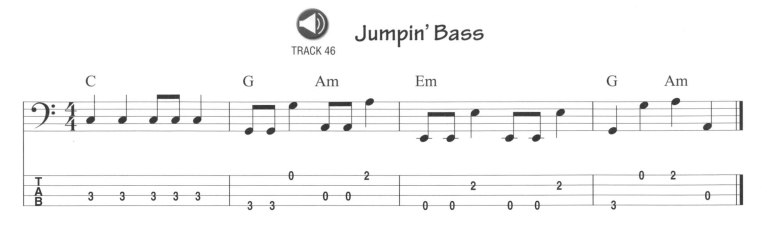

Go slowly at first! Remember the three Ps: patience, practice, and pace yourself.

TRACK 47

## Hard Rocktaves

TRACK 48

## When Johnny Comes Rockin' Home

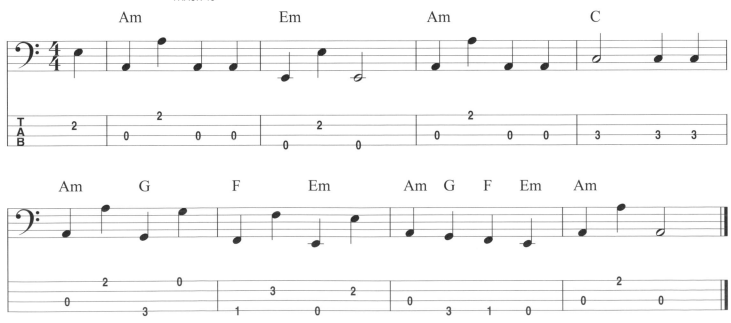

# The Fifth

Remember the major scale pattern? (If not, flip back to page 27.) Five notes up the scale is the **fifth**.

Chords also have fifths. Simply count the root note of a chord as "1" and go up the scale to "5" to find any chord's fifth.

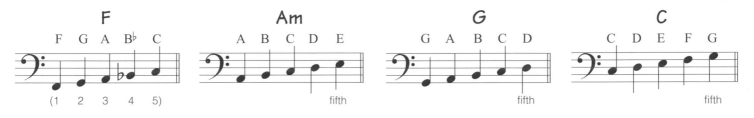

Interchange the root note with the fifth for a really cool sounding bass line:

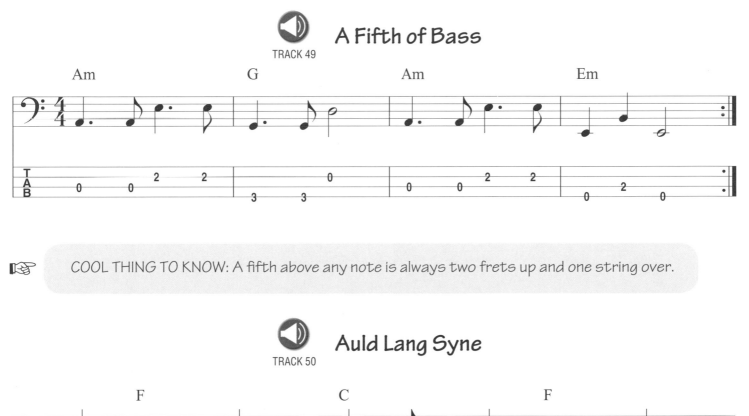

A Fifth of Bass

TRACK 49

☞ COOL THING TO KNOW: A fifth above any note is always two frets up and one string over.

Auld Lang Syne

TRACK 50

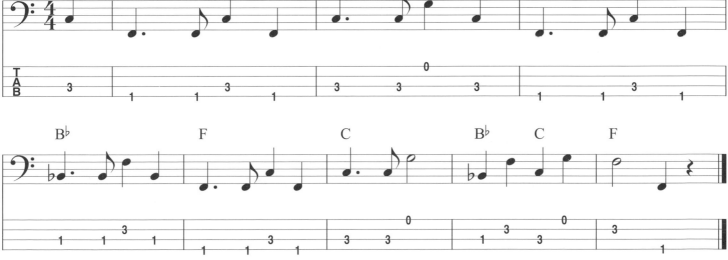

You can also play the fifth **below** the chord's root. For example, C's fifth is G. You can play G above C, or G below C:

☞ COOL THING TO KNOW: The easy part of playing the fifth below the root is that it's on the same fret as the root (only it's one string lower):

## Pop Punk
TRACK 51

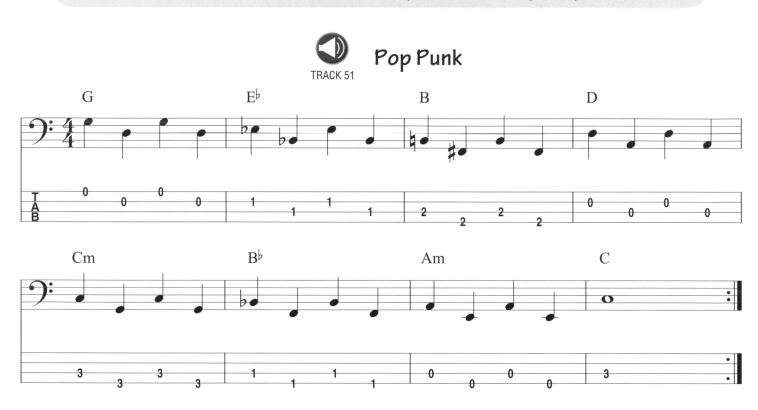

## Greensleeves
TRACK 52

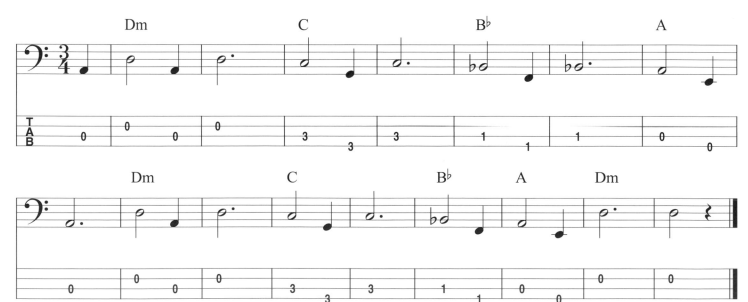

Try mixing roots, fifths, and octaves (and a few notes in between)...

## Rock Groove
TRACK 53

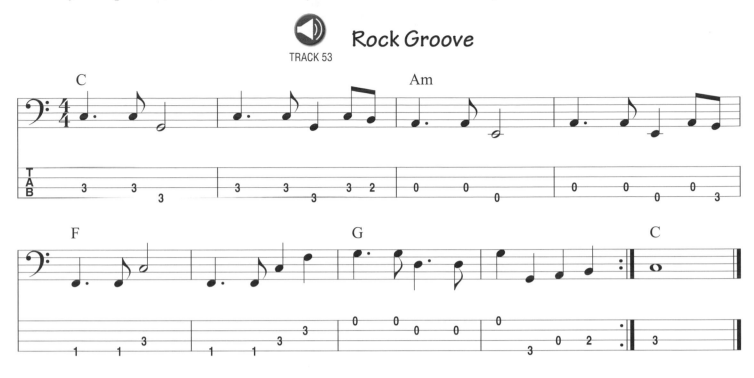

Remember to watch the music, NOT your fingers!

## Scarborough Fair
TRACK 54

# LESSON 9
## *Movin' on up...*

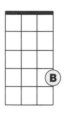 re you still in tune? Relaxed? Ready for even more notes?

**Notes on fret 4**

Wake up finger 4 and stretch it up to fret 4 on each string to learn the following new notes:

 On string 1, fret 4 is "high B":

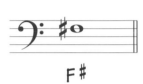

B

 On string 2, fret 4 is F-sharp (your second F-sharp):

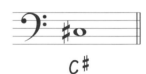

F#

 String 3, fret 4 is C-sharp:

C#

 String 4, fret 4 is G-sharp:

G#

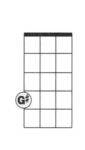 **Fourth Fret Jam**

TRACK 55

## Rockin' Sharps

TRACK 56

Now is a good time to check your tuning.

## Private Eye Groove

TRACK 57

If you're going to play up high for a while, you can do so without stretching finger 4…

## Second Position

Slide your hand up the neck of your bass so that finger 1 is positioned at fret 2. On string 1, finger 1 now plays A, finger 3 plays "high B" and finger 4 learns a new note…

Fret 5 is "high C," written on one leger line above the staff:

C

Now try out your new note (in second position)…

## High C Shuffle

TRACK 58

**NOTE:** fret 5 on the other three strings is the same note as the next open string. Depending on the nature of the song, you can choose whether to play these three notes on an open string or fret 5.

Here is yet another major scale with your new "high C":

## C Major Scale

TRACK 59

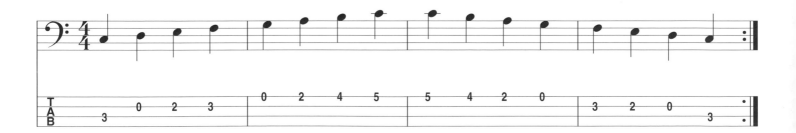

# YOU GOT THE BLUES

Another scale pattern that you'll be glad we taught you is the **blues scale**. Listen to the track, then try playing a blues scale with C as the root note:

### Blues Scale Pattern

TRACK 60

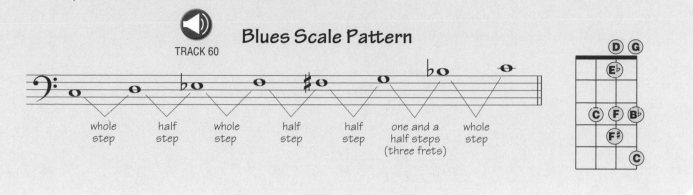

Commit this scale pattern to memory! Use the pattern, or just parts of it, to create some excellent-sounding riffs on any root note…

### Funky Blues

TRACK 61

### Fast Blues

TRACK 62

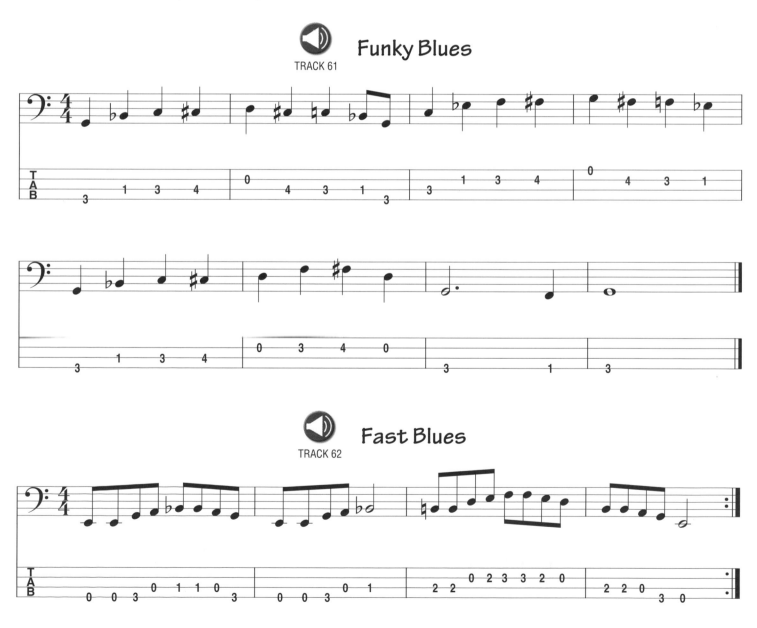

# LESSON 10

## *Time for some music theory...*

A song based on the C major scale is in the **key** of C. Since the C major scale has no sharps or flats, songs and riffs in the key of C also have no sharps or flats:

### Heartland Rock

TRACK 63

Similarly, songs in the key of G are based on the G major scale, which has one sharp—the F-sharp you learned on string 2, fret 4:

### G Major Scale

TRACK 64

**FINGERING TIP:** Instead of stretching, try the scale again with your hand in second position. You'll also find it easier to use second position to play riffs in the key of G.

Rather than have a symbol by every sharp in a song, a **key signature** can be used at the beginning of each line to indicate which notes are sharp throughout the song. For example, the key of G has one sharp, so its key signature will have a sharp on the F-line, telling you to play all Fs as F-sharp.

The next tune's in the key of G (notice the key signature), so use second position for ease and comfort:

## Rockin' in G

TRACK 65

No key signature means the key of C:

## Worried Blues

TRACK 66

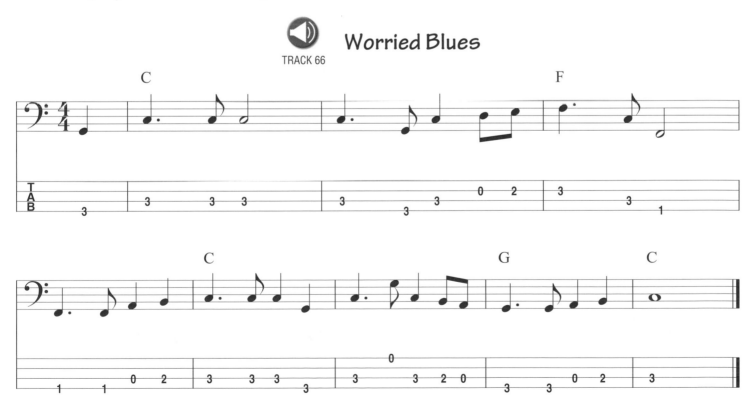

So, if no key signature means the key of C and one sharp means the key of G, how 'bout a key signature with one flat? That's the key of F, based on the F major scale (back on page 26)…

## Rockin' Up the Board

TRACK 67

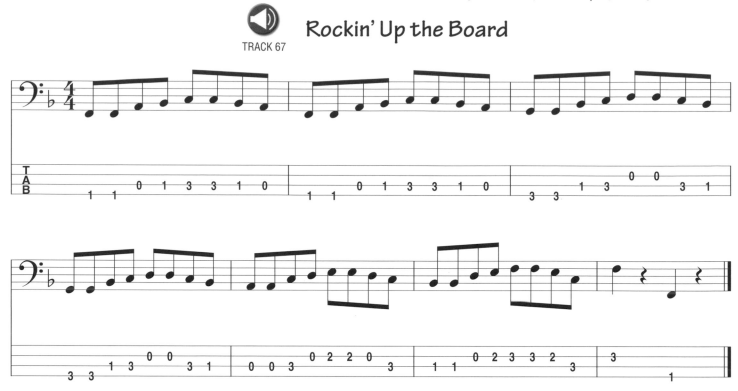

HELPFUL HINT: Let your eyes read ahead of the note that you're actually playing.

## Good Night, My Fans

TRACK 68

CAUTION: You are nearing the end of this book.
Run to your local music dealer, and buy **FastTrack Bass Songbook 1**!

# EVERYTHING AND THE KITCHEN SYNC...

Finally, let us tell you about one of the most essential (and fun) rhythmic concepts in music...

## Syncopation

Syncopation is simply playing notes "off the beat." It makes the music sound less predictable. Listen to a non-syncopated example:

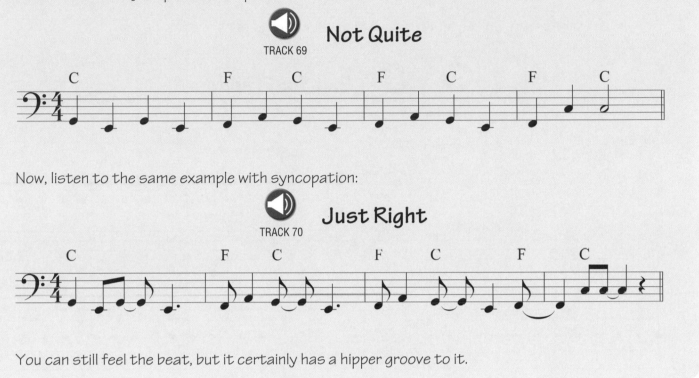

You can still feel the beat, but it certainly has a hipper groove to it.

Try playing this bass line with syncopation. Stress the notes that have an **accent** mark "**>**" above them (most of which will not be on the downbeat)...

# LESSON 11

## *Time to charge admission...*

This isn't really a Lesson...it's a jam session! All the *FastTrack* books (guitar, keyboard, bass, and drums) have the same last section. This way, you can either play by yourself along with the audio or form a band with your friends.

So, whether the band's on the audio tracks or in your garage, let the show begin…

**TRACK 72** full band     **TRACK 73** minus bass     **Exit for Freedom**

TRACK 76
full
band

TRACK 77
minus
bass

# Billy B. Badd

Bravo! Encore!!
*Remember to practice often and always try to learn more about your instrument.*

# WAIT! DON'T GO YET!

Even though we hope (and expect) that you will review this entire book again and again, we thought you might like a "cheat sheet," referencing all the notes you learned.

**Notes on the bass:**

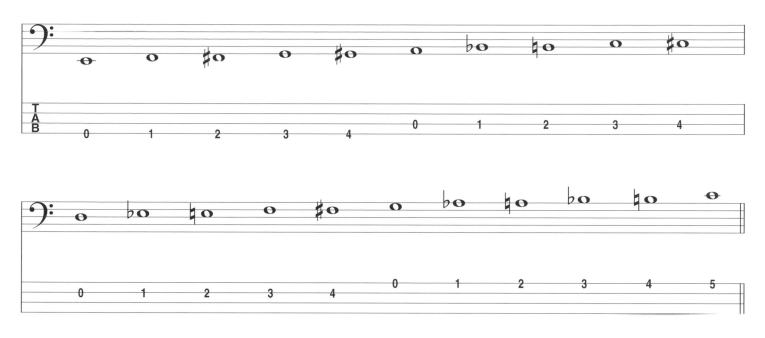

## Conclusion

*"Where do I go now?"*

Here are some suggestions to help you continue to master the bass:

 **Repetition is the best way to learn.** Review the exercises in this book again and again until all the notes and scales are easily playable without even thinking about them.

**2** Buy *"FastTrack Bass: Book 2,"* which teaches many more notes, techniques, and music fundamentals.

**3** Buy *"FastTrack Bass: Songbook 1,"* an excellent book of classic tunes by the Beatles, Clapton, Hendrix, Elton John, and more!

**4** **Enjoy what you do**. Whether it's practicing, riffing, jamming, or even cleaning your bass, do it with a smile on your face. Life's too short.

See you next time...

# SONG INDEX